After Suicide
Help for the Bereaved

Sheila Clark F.R.A.C.G.P.

with contributions by
Diana, Graeme, Kate, Marg and Sandi.

Foreword by Mal McKissock.

HILL OF CONTENT
Melbourne

First published in Australia 1995
by Hill of Content Publishing Company Pty Ltd
86 Bourke Street
Melbourne 3000 Australia
Reprinted 1998

Designed and typeset in Australia
by Geoffrey Robertson
Photography: Mike Annese / Chris Otto

Printed in Australia by
Australian Print Group Maryborough Victoria

National Library of Australia
Cataloguing-in-Publication data

Clark, Sheila Elizabeth.
  After suicide : help for the bereaved.

  Bibliography.
  ISBN 0 85572 262 2.
  1. Bereavement - Phychological aspects. 2. Grief -
  Psychological aspects. 3. Suicide - Psychological aspects.
  4. Suicide victims - Family relationships. I. Title.

155.937

This book is dedicated to

all of you who have lost someone you love

through suicide,

and to

Richard, Cameron, David, Neil and Joel

whose influences still live on.

Acknowledgments

I could not have written this book without the experiences passed on to me by the many people I encountered through the Bereaved Through Suicide Support Group in Adelaide. I thank them for sharing their pain and teaching me so much. In particular, I wish to thank Diana, Graeme, Kate, Marg and Sandi for their special help.

There are many others who have contributed in various forms and whom I wish to thank. Mr Harold Jones was instrumental in initiating this book by listening to me and giving me this task. The other members of the Group's Professional Advisory Council provided assistance from their own areas of expertise: Mr Bevan Craig, Mrs Anne Graham, Professor Robert Goldney, Dr Graham Martin, Mr Tony Monte and Mr Greg Rice.

A number of people reviewed the manuscript and offered helpful comments: Mrs Anne Marley, Dr John Marley, Ms Kate Treharne, the Rev Baldwin Van der Linden, Dr Christopher Wurm, Fr Andrew Zerafa SJ, and the various State coroner's offices. My thanks to Jamie Anderson who did a wonderful job editing my raw text and making the book so readable.

Christopher and Wendy Pullin provided us a retreat during the final preparation of the book.

The University of Adelaide assisted in the production of the manuscript, in particular, Sue Hickey, formerly of the Department of Community Medicine, and Leanne Bragg and Lisa Cameron of the Department of General Practice. My sister, Pat Swell, researched support groups in the United Kingdom.

The following have given permission to quote: Aaron for 'Reflection'; Beacon Press for 'Man's Search for Meaning' by Viktor Frankl; William Heineman Ltd for 'The Prophet' by Kahlil Gibran, 'The Prelude' by William Wordsworth and 'Ulysses' by Alfred Lord Tennyson; National Association for Loss and Grief (New South Wales) for 'Helping the Bereaved'.

And not least, I thank my family, Bruce, Elizabeth, Rebecca and Abigail for all the hours they have spared me.

CONTENTS

Foreword by Mal McKissock   i

Reflection by Aaron   v

1   Beginnings...   1

2   Why did my loved one take their life?   3

3   Why didn't I see it coming?   7

4   It is possible to survive!   9

5   Why don't others grieve as I do?   11

6   How do I work through my grief?   15

7   The grief journey   19

8   The grief map   25

9   Understanding your emotions: 29

     Shock - disbelief - horror & fantasies
why? - guilt - fear - blame from others
- rejection - anger - shame - unfinished
business - legacy of the past - crisis of
values - loss of trust - isolation - sense
of loss - mood changes - suicidal
thoughts - quest for positives
- creating a new life - rebuilding self.

10   A wasted life? Creating purpose   55
     - turning loss into gain

11   What has happened to my beliefs?   63

12   Self care - health care   67

13   Some practical points   77

14   Some business and financial points   85

15   You are not alone - some facts about suicide   89

16   Finally...   93

Suicide bereavement support groups   95

Resource list   99

Information leaflets for family and friends   105

Foreword

The mental anguish and despair following the death of someone we love is often chaotic, unpredictable and unfamiliar in its passionate intensity.

At this time, when bereaved people are questioning their own sanity and ability to survive, it is hard to believe that grief is a natural and healthy response to loss. It is not an illness, and does not need 'treatment'.

The outward expression of grief takes many forms. It depends, too, on our own character: our personality before we were bereaved, the relationship we had with the person who has died, messages we received as children about expressing feelings and the kind of support that is available.

When death has occurred through suicide, social stigma, fear, blame and our own guilt may affect the support that is offered and our responses. Most people feel lonely and alone at some time during their grieving and these feelings are intensified if the bereaved person feels stigmatised or blamed.

Adjusting to life without the person who has died can seem a long and arduous task, and one which is even more difficult if it has to be faced alone. Dr Clark has written this book so that people bereaved by suicide will feel validated, supported and informed about the resources which may help when their need is greatest.

Many bereaved people are tempted to ease their grief with alcohol, analgesics or prescription tranquillisers and sleeping tablets. While these may provide temporary relief, prolonged use of any mood-altering substance inevitably complicates the recovery process physically and emotionally.

As Dr Clark suggests, bereavement counselling and/or support groups can be a healthy alternative. Talking to virtual strangers about an intense personal experience may at first seem unfamiliar or unappealing but it is worth remembering that throughout history people in pain have used counsellors and support groups. Tribal elders have traditionally carried out the functions of 'counsellor'. 'Healing circles' have often provided important rituals of recovery and reintegration into social life. We are basically herd animals and seem to deal with adversity better when we don't have to 'go it alone'.

Story telling is an important part of the recovery process. It is important to be able to tell over and over again the events leading up to and surrounding the death, as well as the effect of the death on the life of the bereaved person.

People may ask about the suicide, for a range of reasons including curiosity, but it is rare to be asked to tell about the life of the person who has died. When someone cares enough to say 'tell me about him/her' we are able to re-experience their life, and the high and low points we have shared with them. In so doing, we gradually decrease the intensity of our pain and, as Dr Clark writes, 'the memories become your treasures'.

As time goes on, you may find you are missing information that you need. You may need to question the police, ambulance, doctors, nurses or funeral director. In my experience, they have been very willing to provide any information they can, and to talk sensitively about their experience of the death or surrounding events.

People close to you may try to discourage you from asking questions in the belief that 'you will only upset yourself'.

Your need to find out whatever you can is normal and healthy. The 'upset' that you feel as you do so is there because someone you care about has suicided, not because you are asking questions.

No matter how co-operative the police, ambulance officers and others are, some questions may remain unanswerable: "why did they do it?". Professional support can help us to live with such unanswerable questions.

Each bereaved person's needs are particular; there is no universal prescription for survival, and certainly none that will take away the pain of separation from someone you love.

However, there are those who can accompany you on your journey through grief so that you don't have to feel so alone.

As you read Dr Clark's book you may find that different points are important at different times. If you follow some of the 'signposts' she highlights, your journey may seem less difficult and your destination more within reach.

Mal McKissock,
Bereavement C.A.R.E. Centre
41 The Boulevarde
Lewisham
New South Wales

Reflection

Composed and read at the funeral of Joel by his brother.

He is our little brother, he is our big brother, he is our sister and our mother and father. He is our closest of friends and a complete stranger. He is our enemy and our ally, anger and joy, sorrow and indifference. He is confusion. He is a tattoo that can never be removed.

He is the air we breathe, the birds in the sky; the earth on which we tread and all the creatures great and small which roam it. He is the sea, the rivers and the lakes and the rain and the life within them. He is the sun and the moon and the stars, the wind in the trees and the trees themselves. As a branch that can no longer hang on, breaks and falls to the ground in the storm, the branch becomes part of the earth, becomes part of us. He is all things.

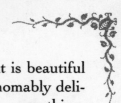

The way of the world is as cruel as it is beautiful and the scales of the universe are so unfathomably delicate. Life means nothing and yet it means everything. We are all part of a never-ending circle in which there are only two guarantees, death and change.

One of the greatest truths is that life is suffering. It is one of the greatest truths because once we truly see this truth we transcend it. Once we truly know that life is suffering and we accept this, then life no longer is suffering. Once it is accepted, the fact that it is difficult no longer matters. Things that hurt, instruct, and it is only through knowing pain and loss that we recognise the unexplainable phenomenon of love. Love is too large, too deep ever to be truly understood or measured or limited within the framework of words.

I will not even attempt to describe the feelings my family and friends had and have for my brother, our brother, our son. But love is risk and love is pain. Love anything that lives and it will die. The price of love is pain. If we are not determined to risk pain then we must do without many things: getting married, having children, the ecstasy of sex, the hope of ambition, friendship, joy and love - all that makes life alive, meaningful and significant.

Change in any dimension, and pain as well as joy will be your reward. A full life will be full of pain and joy at any given moment. The essence of life is change.

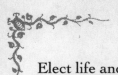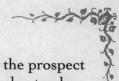

Elect life and growth and you elect change, the prospect of death. Fear not that which you do not understand.

If we can live with the knowledge that death is our constant companion travelling on our left shoulder, then death can become our ally, still fearsome but continually a source of wisdom. With death's counsel, the constant awareness of the limit of our time to live and love, we can always be guided to make the best use of our time and live life to the fullest.

When we shy away from death, the ever-changing nature of things, we inevitably shy away from life. So in death has Joel, our brother, our son and pupil become life, father, mother and teacher.

When you are unhappy look deep into your heart and you shall see that in truth you are weeping for that which has been your delight. It is the loss which is hardest to come to terms with.

Errors and mistakes only exist in the eyes of man but as regards the universe they never existed and never will. On their own level errors are what they are, but the last word will remain with the silence of the constantly evolving universe.

In his confusion Joel may not have realised the magnitude of his actions, but from chaos comes order and from confusion, harmony.

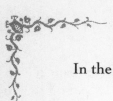

In the words of Kahlil Gibran:

For what is it to die but to stand naked in the wind and to melt into the sun?

And what is it to cease breathing, but to free the breath from its restless tides, that it may rise and expand and seek God unencumbered?

Only when you drink from the river of silence shall you indeed sing.

And when you have reached the mountain top, then you shall begin to climb.

And when the earth shall claim your limbs, then you shall truly dance.

The feeling of loss my family, my sister, my mother and father and I feel is indescribable, as is the intensity of our passion. Do not wait to feel such pain to realise the beauty of what we have and what surrounds us. Life can be so incredibly unfair and there are questions which will never be answered. Unfortunately history cannot be reversed. Time keeps slipping into the future; things happen for reasons only known to the forces of the universe, try not to explain them, only go with them. Go beyond love and grief, exist for the good of man.

We're proud of you Joel. Goodbye and hello.

Aaron

1
Beginnings . . .

Someone you love and cared for has taken their life. You may be left feeling devastated. You may have feelings of shock, disbelief and horror. Why did they do it? Could I have prevented it?

All these and innumerable other emotions may overwhelm you, leaving you hurt, helpless and confused. At times you may even question whether you are going mad. You may wonder whether you or your family are the only people in the world experiencing such trauma. All these thoughts are very normal.

You are not alone. Many people before you have faced the same crisis and survived. This book is compiled from their experiences.

Death through suicide may deeply affect not only the closest family and friends. It also brings pain to more distant relatives and acquaintances, such as grandparents, cousins, friends, teachers, fellow workers, and counsellors.

This book has been written in response to many cries for help from people who have been bereaved through suicide. It is intended to give you some understanding of your grief and to help you to live again fully. It may also help others around you to understand your needs.

2
Why did my loved one take their life?

This is often a burning question giving rise to many emotions. It is common to experience intense feelings of guilt and to blame other people or circumstances.

There are many theories about why people take their lives.

The sociological model

This model focuses on stresses, such as pressures on young people to perform at school, meeting the expectations of adolescence, finding jobs, forming relationships, difficulties in the work place, unemployment, and financial and family worries. As life advances, retirement, redundancy, illness and feelings of uselessness and loss are thought to play a part.

The personality theory

Personality has also been implicated. Suicide has caused the death of many morally aware, sensitive, caring, artistic and perfectionist individuals. Gifted artists, writers, poets and musicians have taken their lives. Some examples include, Vincent van Gogh, Virginia Woolf, Tony Hancock and Adam Lindsay Gordon. Was the stress of life too much for these sensitive souls?

Certainly many who take their lives seem to suffer much stress and feel helpless and hopeless. Suicide to them seems a feasible way out. But these theories do not explain why some survive such traumas and others end up taking their lives.

The medical model

Medicine may have found an answer through some very important recent research. It has been shown that nearly all who take their lives are ill. By reviewing the last weeks or days before the suicide, doctors have found evidence that these people have been suffering mental illness, although the signs of this illness may not have seemed evident at the time. A variety of conditions has been implicated; most commonly depression, but also schizophrenia, alcohol and other substance dependence, and personality problems.

New evidence is emerging that suicide may result from illness, as physical as diabetes or asthma, except that it affects the brain. In diabetes, for example, there is a deficiency of a chemical, insulin, and the body cannot manipulate sugar. Prior to suicide, certain chemicals in the brain, called neurotransmitters, are low so that the brain cannot adequately manipulate thoughts.

How the brain functions

Our processes of thinking are carried out in the brain by a series of messages. These are coded as electrical impulses which pass along nerves, as shown in the diagram below.

As you can see, an impulse passes along the length

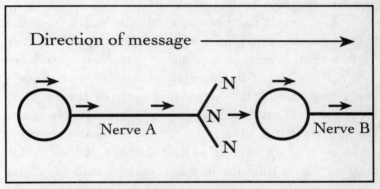

Direction of message

Nerve A

N
N →
N

Nerve B

Transmission of impulses between nerves

of nerve A. When it reaches the end, the nerve sends a signal across the gap to B. It does this by releasing chemicals called neurotransmitters (N), which spread across the gap to stimulate and initiate the impulse in B, and so on.

Clinical depression is caused by disturbances in these neurotransmitters. It has been known for more than thirty years that two of these, adrenalin and noradrenalin, are associated with mood disturbances. Recently, low levels of another, serotonin, have been shown to be important in people who are suicidal.

It is not known entirely what causes depletion of serotonin, but continuous or repeated severe stress is thought to play a part.

A lack of serotonin causes the brain to be unable to function properly and may alter the perception of reality. This may well explain why those who seriously intend to take their lives often experience difficulty in communicating in meaningful terms with their loved ones, in finding alternative solutions and believing in a positive outcome to their problem.

Low levels have been found after death from suicide, whatever the illness suffered beforehand: depression, schizophrenia, alcoholism or personality problems.

What about those suicides that appear to have been impetuous; the seemingly spur of the moment decisions? Low levels of serotonins have also been demonstrated in them. In retrospect many may not have been so impetuous as first thought. Close examination of the time leading up to the death may give clues that indicate the loved one was distressed or making preparations. It may just have been that the behaviour was subtly or inexplicably different. They may have had heart-to-heart conversations or given away some treasured possession as a covert way of saying goodbye. With hindsight, these clues may be easy to see but may not have appeared unusual at the time.

Suicide may be regarded as the consequence of a physical illness affecting the brain, although social and personal factors may also play a part. As yet we have little knowledge of how to diagnose suicide risk before the suicide occurs, but in time and with further research this may be possible.

3

Why didn't I see it coming?

You may be saying to yourself:

*'I've known this person for so long.
I should have seen it coming'.*

Changes in behaviour leading up to suicide are gradual. It is extremely difficult to identify them and to recognise at what point they become significant.

Once a person has made up their mind to take their life, they seem to go to considerable lengths to conceal their distress from those closest to them, because it is they who would be the most likely to discover and interrupt their plans.

Even doctors who specialise in this field have difficulty.

4

It is possible to survive!

Many people feel such intense emotional pain after the suicide of a loved one that they wonder whether they can survive. It certainly is possible to survive as the contributors to this book have found.

You may find it hard to believe now but your grief will not stay the same. It will change as you work through it and you will come to feel more comfortable about your loss. If you so choose, you may grow as a person from the experience and integrate that experience into your existence and create a more meaningful life for yourself and others. In effect, the influence of your loved one will still live on.

5

Why don't others grieve as I do?

It is normal for different people to grieve in different ways, but this often gives rise to a lot of misunderstanding.

Some people avoid talking about their loved one for fear of upsetting others. They then find themselves isolated. A pretence may be built up that the loved one did not exist. This can be painful, and many people yearn to talk freely about their loved one, to feel their existence had some significance. Families who have been able to share their grief together have found this comforting and supportive; sharing has often strengthened the family unit and helped the influence of the loved one to live on. However this may not always be possible. Not all families can be so open.

Some people think their grief is too private to talk about. They may be afraid to reveal their true emotions and fear outbursts of tears and being thought weak. They may worry that the intensity of their grief is abnormal.

Invite them to talk by telling them how you feel, either verbally or by letter. Leave your diary describing your feelings open for them to see. They will then not feel there is something wrong with them.

It is normal for some not to want to talk but comforting for them to know that you are around.

How may different relationships affect grief?

A mother may feel her grief differently from a father because of the physical bonding she had with the child.

A father's experience:

'It shits me off that few other men are prepared to admit the depth of the pain'.

A brother's experience:

'I don't feel I've lost a brother,
I feel I've lost my best friend'.

Brothers and sisters who lose a sibling sometimes feel erroneously that their grief should be less than that of their parents. Girlfriends and boyfriends may feel rejected by the family and the scapegoat of the suicide.

Young people tend to underestimate their needs and are often overlooked. They need space to grieve in their own way. This may be different from that of others.

Mixed families often find the death of a loved one from a previous marriage causes different levels of grief in various individuals. Difficulties arise in understanding the amount of support that is required of each other. Grieving the loss of a previous partner may cause jealousy and misunderstandings in a relationship. You may feel additional loss when you realise your new partner cannot cope with your feelings of grief. You may feel they have let you down. (It is hard for the new partner too.)

Other family, friends and associates may also have deep feelings of grief and not understand why they feel passionate emotions. They, too, have lost someone they care for and naturally feel distress.

Sexual desires may alter following a bereavement. The libido swings wildly. If not understood, this may cause stress in relationships.

6
How do I work
through my grief?

You may wonder what you have to do to get through your grief. The grief process is like a journey running from the starting point of your bereavement to a new life. Your journey can be seen as a line on a map.

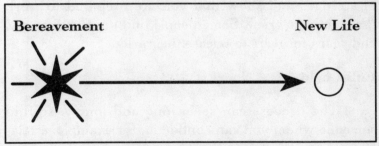

Grief journey 1

You will progress through your grief as you work through your feelings. Freud called this grief work.

Grief time

Allow yourself a fifteen to twenty minute grief period every day. Make sure you can be alone and have put on the answering machine so you won't be disturbed. This time acts as a safety valve. In it you can deal with any emotions that you have stored up.

You may wish to use different ways of grieving at these times: thinking, crying, praying, meditating, writing or drawing.

You may like to keep a diary. Write down your feelings, your grief and the memories of your loved one. You will then notice how your grief changes over a period of weeks and months. This will be proof to you of your progress. Keep the diary in a safe place; the memories you have written down about your loved one will be precious for you in the future.

Alternatively you may feel more comfortable with pictures or diagrams.

Many people find crying a relief. Rather than being an indication of weakness, tears are often a sign of strength and show that you are prepared to work through your grief. Some people find it difficult to cry, and yearn for tears to release their grief.

Enlist help

The process can seem long and lonely, so find someone whom you can confide in, for example, a relative or friend.

If you have difficulty finding someone suitable, your doctor or local community health centre may be able to help in this way, or refer you on to a specialist grief counsellor. Some people find the experience of someone else who has been through a similar situation invaluable, so a list of suicide support groups is included at the back of this book.

> ## GRIEF ASSISTANCE
>
> *Family*
> *Friends*
> *Counsellor*
> *Pet*
> *Support group*
> *Diary*
> *Drawings*
> *Prayer*

7
The grief journey

Initially . . .

At first you may be overcome with shock and confusion. You may feel guilty. It may all seem like a bad dream. You may find you can live only minute by minute, day to day. You may have had to deal with the police, coroner's officials and funeral directors at a very private time of your life. You may have to communicate with your loved one's place of work or education and deal with questions from friends and neighbours. What should I tell them? Do I try to cover up the suicide? (See 'Shame' in chapter 9 and 'What to tell others' in chapter 13.)

After the funeral . . . unreality . . .

After the funeral you may wonder why your grief gets worse instead of better. You may feel the separation from your loved one becomes more painful after parting with the physical body. Your loved one may feel very distant from you.

You may be struggling with the unreality of the death every time you face a new situation which would have involved your loved one. You may find yourself faced repeatedly with the pain that they will not return.

Three to four months . . .

After about three or four months you may reach a low point in your grief as the reality that your loved one is not coming back sinks in fully. Many people find this very hard to accept. It takes some much longer than others. You may find yourself fighting against it, crying out, and yearning and pining.

You may be frightened of losing the memories of your loved one and be temporarily unable to visualise their face. You will never lose those memories. They just become hidden for a while and will re-emerge later. You will hold on to them and they will become very precious for you. This is one way your loved one will be with you now. Making the change towards that acceptance can be very difficult.

You may be given constant subtle reminders of your loss. There are no telephone calls and no home-comings. You watch your loved one's friends continuing with their normal lives. Support from family and friends may be diminishing as they have by now moved on through their grief and are getting on with their lives and expect you to do the same. You may be feeling intensely lonely.

You are also probably becoming physically and

emotionally exhausted. It is usual for the body's mechanisms which promote the coping responses to become drained about this time. And, incredibly, most people expect you to be back on your feet by now. This is a good time to visit your doctor. Your health can be assessed and you have an opportunity to discuss any further help.

The grief journey at this time may appear to you to have developed a low point, as shown in the diagram.

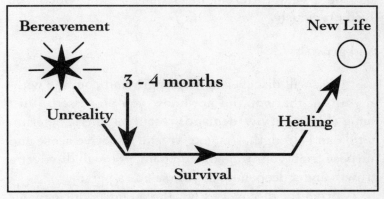

Grief journey 2

But things will not stay this way . . .

Survival . . .

As the days pass you will experience your grief beginning to lift and it may surprise you that life can regain some normality. You will experience good days and bad days; it will be quite normal for you to see-saw up and down between feelings of coping and despair. As time goes on you will experience more peaks and fewer troughs and the troughs will become progressively shallower.

Healing . . .

In the early stages you may find it difficult to believe that your grief will lift and your journey will take an upward turn. The intense pain and sadness which you are feeling will subside and the memory of your loved one will become more comfortable in your mind. You will retain the happy memories. You will invest in life again and plan your future, although this may be a very different life from the one which you lived previously.

And growth

You will discover new strength and courage within yourself that you did not know you possessed. Just being able to survive demands resourcefulness, determination and strength. As you wrestle to derive sense and purpose from your tragedy and pain, you will discover a growth and a deepening of yourself as a person.

From the discoveries which you make during your grief journey, will come a new sense of purpose and creativity in your life. Different people find this in different ways: caring for others, accomplishing some task, perfecting some skill, having a greater sensitivity to nature or in developing their personal philosophy. You will have changed and your life will have changed too. It takes time to accept the new you.

I am a part of all that I have met;

Yet all experience

is an arch wherethro'

Gleams that untravelled world,

whose margin fades

Forever and forever when I move.

'Ulysses' Alfred Lord Tennyson

The grief map

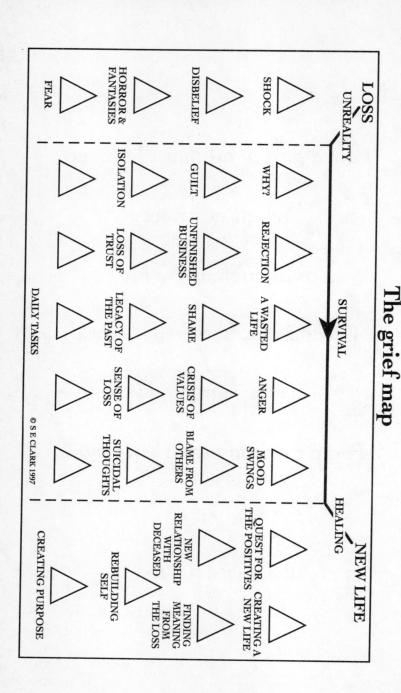

© S E CLARK 1997

24

8
The grief map

By now you are probably experiencing a host of emotions, and asking yourself a lot of questions. You may feel confused and overwhelmed. In order to help you sort out these feelings, the common emotions following a suicide bereavement are shown on the map opposite. You may not experience all of them so cross off those that do not relate to you. Others may be particular to you, so the blanks are for you to name.

One can become overwhelmed and confused not only because there are so many emotions but also because these emotions are so difficult to face. It is helpful to imagine that each emotion and question is a mountain that you are climbing.

Some mountains may require a supreme effort rather like scaling a rock face. At times you feel yourself slipping backwards. You may succeed in climbing to the peak of a problem only to discover another, even higher one, ahead.

At times it may be difficult to see where you are going and how far you have come. You may feel caught in the undergrowth because you are dealing with an emotion which is particularly difficult for you. As in climbing a mountain, there may be alternative ways to the top; when dealing with your emotions it is important to find the path which suits you.

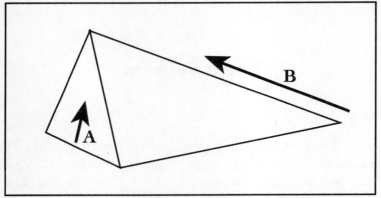

Mountain paths of suicide bereavement

Some paths are very steep (A). An easier path is found by looking at the mountain from a different aspect (B). It takes time to find the best path; you need to seek different types of advice to help you.

Mark which mountains you are climbing at present. Give yourself credit; mountaineering demands courage, strength and resourcefulness. It is hard work. Don't forget every mountaineer deserves a rest at times.

Just as when approaching the top of a mountain you see a view, so when you are completing a climb up an emotional mountain, you will develop a new perspective of your situation.

Everyone experiences grief in their own way. There is no one right way. You will tend to experience the emotions of unreality first, followed by survival and healing. You will experience some emotions more intensely and have more difficulty with some than others.

Work through your emotions in your own particular order and in your own combinations. You may return repeatedly to some emotions in an attempt to finish them off. Some you may have to be content to leave unfinished, while you go on to others.

'I feel stuck in my grief'.

This feeling is very normal and is to be expected at times as you work through your grief. Remember the analogy of the mountain. As you grapple with the emotion, you are climbing it. You will then see you are making progress but in a vertical dimension. This will naturally appear to slow down your progress along the horizontal line.

'I'm not coping'.

Carrying on with the necessities of life which you are doing now, such as, eating, dressing, washing and shopping, is evidence you are coping. In normal circumstances these are ordinary activities but under your present circumstances these achievements are quite extraordinary. The fact that you are reading this book shows you have chosen to actively work on your grief.

So, even though the mountain at this stage may

resemble a vertical rock face, you are doing a good job clinging on. If you are tearful, remember, tears are a healthy sign you are dealing with your emotions.

How to use the grief map

1. Underline the mountains relevant to your journey.
2. Cross out those mountains that are not relevant.
3. Are there mountains which do not have the exact name you want? If so, cross out the printed name and put in your own.
4. Are any of your issues not on the map? If so, name these under the blank mountains.
5. Fill in each mountain to the height you perceive you have climbed. For example if you feel you have half dealt with an issue, demonstrate you have climbed that mountain half way by filling in the lower half:

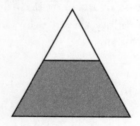

6. Now examine the map.
   What issues have you dealt with?
   What successes can you identify?
   What issues do you need to work on?

   If you need help ask a counsellor or your doctor for assistance.

9

Understanding your emotions

Shock

Perhaps it never occurred to you that your loved one would take their life. Even if you did anticipate it or if they had attempted suicide before, the death itself is a shock. You may have been shocked discovering the body. You may also experience it with increasing realisation of the full meaning of the tragedy.

People act differently in shock. Some 'freeze' and withdraw into themselves. They have difficulty in making decisions and leave tasks to others.

Others respond to the 'fight or flight' mechanism; this is the response to stay and fight or run away. Whoever takes on responsibilities following the death is acting under the influence of fight. Those who busy themselves in other tasks and run away from the reality of the death are driven by the flight instinct.

The shock will sometimes be severe enough to

cause physical symptoms such as nausea, abdominal pain, breathlessness, shaking and faintness. Chest pains should be checked out by your doctor.

Disbelief

Following the suicide you will at times have difficulty believing your loved one is really dead: you feel that they are just away on holiday and will come home soon.

You may expect to hear their voice when you pick up the phone. It all seems like a bad dream from which you will soon wake. It is particularly distressing to grasp that this dream is reality.

Some people feel their loved one is especially close in spirit and take comfort from this. Others find solace from seeing them in dreams.

Disbelief, in its various forms, acts as a natural protective mechanism and helps in the early stages of calamity. The tapering off of this protective mechanism and increasing realisation that the loved one is dead, make grief, to many people, more painful after the initial stages.

Horror and fantasies

The horror of the death will disturb you, especially if you were the first to find the body. Intrusive images of what you saw are sometimes severe enough to be classed as 'Post Traumatic Stress Disorder'. This is a problem over and above the grief. It is a reaction caused by witnessing a shocking event and is often alleviated by special counselling.

Even if you did not see the body your imagination may be running wild; you may be disturbed by your own thoughts, unable to think clearly and be having nightmares. Confide in someone about what you saw or your thoughts about it.

You may imagine the despair which drove your loved one to take their life. Remember, they are now at peace. They have obtained what they wanted. Their problem has been solved.

You may have particular questions about how your loved one died. How much physical suffering was there? Often one's imagination is worse than the reality. Talking with the coroner's officer or your doctor will help. In most countries your doctor can apply, if you request, for a copy of the coroner's report. When this becomes available you can go through it together. The coroner's office will provide such information to the next of kin.

Now your loved one is no longer around you feel as though part of you is missing. Just as an amputee experiences feelings in the missing limb, so you experience fantasies that your loved one is still here. You are certain you hear their voice or see them in the street. You worry that others will think you are hallucinating; that you are going mad. No, you are not. These are normal fantasies which persist for a while after a bereavement.

Why?

Why did this disaster happen to you and your loved one? You may wonder why God or fate allowed it. Some people, erroneously, think the suicide is a punishment for something they have done in the past.

You also search for why your loved one took their life and their state of mind before they died. You may find the answers difficult to obtain. Many people never fully understand the emotions or causes leading to their loved one's suicide. Many find that in trying to answer the question they encounter feelings of guilt.

It helps to talk to those who knew your loved one and anyone who was with them in the time leading up to the death. Again, the coroner's report and talking to coroner's officials may help.

As mentioned earlier, it is important to remember the evidence that suicide may be caused by a low level of serotonin in the brain. Most of those who take their lives are suffering an illness which causes their thinking to be restricted and their view of the situation to be very different from reality. They perceive their situation to be hopeless and are helpless at asking for assistance. If help is offered they do not understand that it will be useful. It may seem that they and their helpers are speaking different languages that neither party can understand. Communication breaks down. As a result your loved one even blames - perhaps in a suicide note - those who have tried most to help.

Once someone has made up their mind to take their own life, it appears there is very little anyone can do. Even professionals specialising in the field cannot always prevent a suicide.

The suicide note

The disturbed mind of the writer means that any message is often a poor guide to the reason for suicide.

Sometimes one or more people are singled out for blame in the note. As a result, they may suffer enormous guilt.

It is normal to blame and be angry at those with whom one feels closest and most comfortable, family for example, because of the safety and forgiveness which come from close relationships. Your loved one, in blaming you, may have been displaying confidence in you.

Similarly, some suicide notes in which thanks are expressed, omit the names of the nearest and dearest. People often take for granted those who are closest to them and omission from the note may well indicate that the loved one had great security and confidence in the relationship.

Some final messages express beautiful sentiments and become everlasting treasures.

Guilt

You have probably said to yourself many times over:

'If only I had done this . . .'

'If only I hadn't done that . . .'

Guilt can be one of the most difficult and distressing emotions; you may feel guilty for not having been able to save your loved one from taking their life. The regrets you experience are deeply painful. Many people worry that they could not identify the suicidal behaviour. They did not realise that giving away favourite possessions or heart-to-heart talks were ways of saying goodbye.

Guilt may come from aspects of your relationship with your loved one. Parents often feel guilty about their parenting, sometimes to the extent of feeling failures as parents. Brothers and sisters may feel strong responsibility, particularly if there has been the very normal sibling rivalry. Spouses may feel that they have been inadequate particularly as confidants and in providing support.

When someone is contemplating taking their life they often become secretive to conceal their plan, particularly from those closest to them, for fear of being discovered.

There may have been considerable disharmony and disruption of relationships before the death. The quality of relationship is often on trial following the suicide. But bereaved people may feel too guilty to be able to judge accurately.

Sometimes memories of wishing the person dead in times of severe disharmony causes anguish. These are normal thoughts at times and you should not hold these against yourself.

Families and friends of those who have made repeated suicide attempts may feel guilt at feelings of relief that the suicide is finally accomplished.

You may feel guilt at being the survivor, particularly if blamed by others.

You may feel guilty at being unable to help others in their grief and at finding it difficult to cope yourself.

Some feel guilty at experiencing such deep grief. They underrate the importance of the relationship with the loved one.

Coping with guilt . . .

Unless it is dealt with carefully, guilt can be one of the most destructive emotions.

Initially, bereaved people find it difficult to realise that much of the guilt is imagined and unrealistic. They mistakenly believe they should have been totally responsible for and in control of the life of their loved one.

With hindsight it is too easy to criticise what you have or have not done. Remember;

> *You acted with the information you had* **AT THE TIME.**

Often survivors are emotionally distraught and their memories play tricks. These thought pathways can be dangerous.

Confide in someone with whom you feel secure. Contact a support group; talk with someone who has had a similar bereavement. See how they coped with feelings of guilt.

If you cannot share your feelings of guilt, record them in some way. For example write them down; tape them, or express them in drawings or art. This may relieve your burden.

Review what you have done and imagine you are an observer, outside yourself. As you go over your recorded feelings again, test yourself on the questions on the following page:

> • *How much of my guilt is imagined?*
> *Look at yourself with the knowledge*
> *you had at the time.*
> • *Have I allowed any blame from*
> *others to be laid on me?*
> • *Am I whipping myself with guilt*
> *to punish myself? Why?*

If you allow yourself to be too consumed by guilt you will have insufficient time and energy to look at other aspects of your grief. It may be more beneficial to turn your attention to deriving meaning from your grief experience. Look, too, at ways of perpetuating the influence of your loved one (see chapter 10).

Fear

You may also experience feelings of anxiety or foreboding of another catastrophe, and feel generally insecure. You may feel safer within the confines of your own home and have difficulty in leaving it to go shopping or to work.

Anxieties crop up such as fear for the safety of remaining family members. You become overprotective of them. You also experience fear of facing the future without your loved one, and of how you will cope.

You will become more confident. At first, it will help to have support from someone who has been through a similar experience or is familiar with the difficulties. Contact with a support group, or a counsellor can be useful.

Blame from others

Others may appear to blame you for your loved one's death. You feel alienated, alone, unsupported and often angry.

Maybe you have lost your partner and the partner's family is blaming you. You find this difficult, as you may be yearning for contact with the next of kin and their support in your grief.

Blame is the only way some people can manage their own grief. They are hurting very much too and try to protect themselves this way. Be patient. Keep all doors of communication open. People later realise with sorrow the devastating effects that their blame has had on others.

Rejection

You may feel your loved one didn't want you any more, and deserted or rejected you. These feelings leave people feeling desperately hurt or even insulted. Some people wonder whether their loved one did it out of spite to get even.

You may feel your loved one chose to do this to you and that this 'choice' makes your grief different. However, they have usually been so absorbed and deeply immersed in their own problems, that they were oblivious of the effects the suicide would have. Their goal was usually to obtain relief from distress.

You may feel your attempts to help your loved one before death were rejected. A disturbed mind is beyond accepting help after the idea of suicide becomes fixed.

Anger

Anger worries many people. It is a reaction they did not expect. Bereaved people often find they have a lot to be angry about: the events or actions which led up to the suicide and at themselves for being unable to prevent it.

You feel angry at the hurt and disruption that has come into your life, at the pain of your loss, the blame and stigma.

You may even feel anger towards your loved one; at the rejection, for being cheated out of the relationship, at having to assume a new role, for example, earning the family income or caring for the children. You may resent the predicament which has been forced on you. You may be angry at the pain they caused others you love or care for.

You may feel the need to get even with your loved one. You feel that these emotions are wrong when you should be feeling remorse.

Anger can be a part of the healing process. It helps to relieve guilt and the intense sadness. Anger is, in fact, a projection of one's own sadness. When it is directed against the dead loved one, it is a very normal way of acknowledging the suffering brought to the family.

Often there follows eventually an emotional reconciliation which becomes acceptance; an acknowledgment that life can be put in order again, that it is no longer so shaken up; this episode has passed and life has settled down again.

Coping with anger . . .

Anger can be a dangerous emotion and needs to be recognised as such to avoid it causing you harm. It is tempting to put anger to negative use.

When used positively, it can be a valuable source of energy. Harness that energy; allow it to help you. For example, use the energy of your anger in physical activities such as digging the garden. Make it fuel your determination to create a new life. Use it to search for a new purpose from your grief, or to perpetuate the influence of the life of your loved one (chapter 10).

Shame

Suicide is no longer stigmatised by most religions. In progressive countries it is no longer illegal. However, there is still a lot of misunderstanding about suicide and mental illness. It might not be possible to change social attitudes in your lifetime but you can try.

Many bereaved people feel an aura of shame about the suicide which troubles them in unexpected ways.

The first problem encountered is informing others of the death. It may be tempting to hide the truth, but this always leads to complications later. Be as honest as you can about the cause of death without going into details.

There is often a feeling of being talked about and

it may be tempting to withdraw from others. It is important to realise, that with the greater understanding we now have about suicide, there is nothing to be ashamed about.

You may experience shame if you feel you are not coping with your grief. Remember, it is healthy to express your grief. Tears are a sign you are working on your grief. Men are brought up to 'be strong'. They often have more difficulty talking about their feelings than women.

Unfinished business

'I didn't even say goodbye'

There may be many things you were unable to say to your loved one because of the suddenness of the death. Perhaps you wish you had been able to settle old disputes or to put right some misunderstandings. You fear your loved one died feeling unloved and lonely. You may wish to tell them you really cared, and to thank them for all they meant to you. Yearning to communicate these things can be very distressing.

It may help to note down your thoughts in a diary or write a letter to your loved one. Keep the pages somewhere safe, or give them to your loved one by burying them under the headstone or under a bush planted as a memorial.

You might find it helpful to visit the grave and talk to your loved one. Say your goodbyes. Tell them about your feelings for them. Don't worry about being seen and thought stupid. Stay until you feel comfortable. Try to resist the urge to run away.

Legacy of the past

You may have had weeks, months or even years of troubled times before your loved one took their life. You felt uneasy about aspects of their life; their moods or behaviour. There may have been disharmony in your relationship with them. This may have upset the whole family. You found it difficult to communicate and to understand their thoughts and actions. Some people have described the difficulty in communicating to be as if the loved one were speaking a foreign language.

Remember that these may be symptoms of their mental illness and of the difficulty in processing thoughts in which low levels of serotonin play a part. Such behaviour may have appeared normal to you at the time. It is often difficult to recognise that anything is wrong when problems develop gradually in someone close.

You may grieve for these lost times and for the unfulfilled relationship. You feel guilt or anger about their effect on you and the family.

Those who have cared for their loved one, knowing they were disturbed, sometimes have feelings of relief or failure.

You may worry, too, that in caring for the loved one, there were others in the family whom you neglected. These are normal discoveries. Now is the time to concentrate on these relationships.

Crisis of values

Many people feel their self esteem plummet following the suicide of a loved one. They doubt their own values and philosophies of life: the priorities they gave to family love, work, friendships, integrity, education and religion.

You may feel insecure and mistrust your own judgement. You find it hard to make decisions. You see no meaning or purpose in your life any more. It can be distressing to lose one's certainty. Remember the earlier analogy of the mountain; it is often difficult to see the top when you are struggling in the undergrowth. But the summit does not go away; it is just waiting for you to sight it again.

Although difficult to believe at this stage, the undergrowth does become thinner as you climb. You will again see where you are heading.

Loss of trust

You may feel your loved one betrayed the mutual trust of your relationship. You feel deceived by the secrecy of the suicide. You may then be afraid to invest in new relationships even though they would provide very important help at this time.

Isolation

Bereavement alters relationships. Having so many negative emotions, you are tempted to avoid contact with others. You find friends avoid you, or are awkward in your company. They do not know how to behave, and you may have the additional task of teaching them. For this reason some cut-out information sheets are included in this book to give to your friends and relatives.

You may become isolated within your family circle. Family members find it difficult to talk about the loved one for fear of upsetting each other. You may feel resentful that others do not appear to be grieving much or even not to be grieving at all. You feel that you are the only one hurting so much and that no-one else understands how you feel.

It is normal for people to express their grief in different ways. Try to encourage others to talk about how they feel and encourage them to listen to you. You will be surprised how much you have in common.

There is a real danger of becoming isolated and of denying yourself access to the supports necessary to help you through your bereavement.

Accept offers of help from others in whatever guise they come. Maintain contact and you will feel less isolated. There are others out there wanting to help you. Give them the chance!

Sense of loss

> *'I feel as if someone has torn open my chest*
> *and made a hole in my heart,*
> *leaving an empty space'*

The pain you feel is the result of love, loved; the greater the love, the greater the pain. If this love had meaning in life so it still does in death. Why should we allow death to cut short this love?

As Viktor Frankl wrote:

Love goes very far beyond the physical person of the beloved. It finds its deepest meaning in his spiritual being, his inner self. Whether or not he is actually present, whether or not he is still alive at all, ceases somehow to be of importance.

'Man's Search for Meaning'

Feel the love in your heart, alongside the loss. When you feel the pain, remember the love too; beauty and pain at the one time.

Sadness and yearning will be constantly present at first. These pangs occur less frequently later. These feelings tend to return when least expected and you may be caught off your guard. You may be enjoying yourself when thoughts of your loved one suddenly overwhelm you.

Hold on to the memories of your loved one.

They are precious.

They can help fill the void.

Daily tasks

What have you had to do in your daily life since your loved one died? You may have had to study or go to work, make major decisions, keep the house running, care for the children. Make a list. Give yourself credit for all you have done.

Mood changes

Your mood will see-saw up and down from day to day.

Some people describe the troughs of intense sadness as 'depression'. This is not to be confused with depression, the mental illness, which needs medical help. Some people describe these troughs as if they have fallen down a pit or are in a dark tunnel.

Many people are frightened of the troughs following a suicide. Although it is important to grieve and to give way to your tears and emotions it is also important to prepare some strategies for the occasions when you feel desperately low.

Coping with mood changes . . .

Complete the Emergency Help List, set out in the box on the following page.

List people whom you could visit or ring, even in the middle of the night. Write down any activities you usually find divert your attention. Include, for example, a favourite hobby, music, gardening, radio or television. List some readings you find uplifting and strengthening, such as, poems, and inspirational and religious books. Keep this list safe and use it.

EMERGENCY HELP LIST

People I can ring:

_____

_____

_____

_____

Activities I can do:

DRAWING/PAINTING

Music, piano/saxophone

_____

_____

My helpful readings are:

_____

_____

_____

_____

Suicidal thoughts

After a suicide you may worry about whether other family members or you, yourself, might do the same. Distress at separation from the loved one frequently leads people to briefly contemplate suicide themselves. These thoughts pass as the grieving process proceeds. But, until they do, using the help list you have just made will be useful.

Some people worry about being drawn by fate down the same path as their loved one. This may be particularly so later, when a younger brother or sister reaches the age at which the older one died.

Suicide is not something that happens because of fate, though. It happens at a critical stage in mental illness, when thinking is restricted. Suicide cannot be 'passed down' in a family, but some mental illnesses do run in families. Modern treatments are usually quite effective, particularly if the condition is detected and treated in the early stages. If you are worried about possible suicide involving yourself or another family member, you should seek help from your doctor.

Quest for positives

Throughout your grief you may search for positives. Can you relate to these comments?

'My husband is now at peace'.

'It was my son's decision to take his life'.

'I'm glad I knew her'.

'I know at heart I was a good mother to her'.

'He was a darned good mate'.

'I've learned a lot about myself - thanks'.

'I realised for the first time how much other people care'.

*'Very special things have happened which would never
have happened otherwise'.*

If existence with the loved one was difficult, some people experience relief that the distress is over and life can settle down and get better. Those who suffered repeated threats to self-destruct from their loved one may feel relief that suicide is no longer a threat.

List the positives you recognise have come out of the situation.

POSITIVES

_____

_____

_____

_____

_____

Creating a new life

You have, in fact, been creating a new life ever since the suicide. Make a list now of all the things you have done since, however small. You have had to survive physically. You have had to cook, eat, wash and work. You have had to carry out some very difficult tasks; breaking the news to others of your loved one's death; attending to their affairs; communicating with the coroner's office; planning the funeral. You may have new family responsibilities. There could be new financial or work considerations. Do not underestimate the size of all these tasks. Give yourself the credit you deserve.

Friendships change. You will make new ones as you experience the different forms of support those around you provide. You will develop different interests and your life may take new directions.

List everything you have done in creating a new life:

MY SUCCESS LIST

_____

_____

_____

_____

cont...

MY SUCCESS LIST *(cont.)*

_____

_____

_____

_____

_____

_____

_____

_____

_____

_____

_____

_____

_____

Rebuilding self

Your self confidence may have become low. Your ability to make decisions may have changed.

Have you made your success list yet? Examine these achievements. What special qualities did you need to achieve them?

MY SPECIAL QUALITIES

_____

_____

_____

_____

_____

_____

_____

You will come to feel good about yourself again. Work on maintaining relationships and making new ones. Give yourself credit for all you have accomplished. Be kind to yourself!

Celebrate your achievements!

You will discover strength

and courage from your grief

that will make you

proud of yourself.

How strange that all

The terrors, pains and early miseries,

Regrets, vexations, lassitudes

interfused

Within my mind, should e'er have

borne a part,

And that a needful part,

in making up

The calm existence that is

mine when I

Am worthy of myself!

'The Prelude'

William Wordsworth

10
A Wasted life?

Creating purpose
- turning loss into gain

Many people feel their loved one's life has been wasted. But:

> *A person's value does not*
> *die with them.*
> *Their influences*
> *and memories remain.*

Remember the times you had together. Get out the photos to remind you. Sometimes the memories become hidden by the pain you feel, but they will return. You now become their guardian. Write them down and keep them safe. These memories can never be taken from you.

What was special about your loved one? Remember what they meant to you. Remember how their life affected you. How would you like that to continue? What values, aspirations, attributes and joys they created would you like to see survive? It helps also to imagine what they would have wished to continue. These are the treasures that now become yours. Remember them with pride and gratitude. It is up to you, now, to nurture them and encourage them to grow. The future influence of your loved one becomes the responsibility of those who were close to them in life.

The process of grieving does not mean moving away from the person who has died but towards a new relationship with them in terms of the meaning they will have for you.

What were the values, aspirations, attributes
and joys of my loved one?

_____

_____

_____

_____

_____

Which would my loved one like me to continue

_____

_____

_____

_____

_____

NOW

REMEMBER THESE WITH
PRIDE AND GRATITUDE.

When someone we love dies or when we are faced with a major loss situation we are confronted with one of the greatest challenges of life. The experiences of life and death which we tap during our grief open up a whole world of new possibilities to us. These will include our decisions about finding meaning from the disaster and the pathways which our future life will take. This presents us with the opportunity to grow beyond ourselves.

Because we are human we are not driven by instincts, but by our own choices. We have the freedom to choose how to face this challenge. This includes the attitudes we adopt in the effort to create meaning and find a new purpose out of the life and out of the death of our loved one.

You can choose to integrate this experience into your life to make something very special to come out of this situation. Answering the following questions will help you find your direction.

How do I wish to grow personally from my grief?

_____

_____

_____

_____

How can I best use the rest of my life?

_____

_____

_____

_____

What would I like to see myself doing in 5 years' time?

_____

_____

You are a unique individual with special qualities (remember the list you made earlier?). You can choose to develop them to create new purpose from your grief. Build on them. Integrate them into your life.

Remember:

> *You are a unique individual*
>
> *with special qualities.*

After tragedy, some people develop greater sensitivity to the needs of others. They become more caring, or work for the benefit of others. Some become more creative. Others, through experiencing the beauty of nature, art, truth or loving relationships have a richer, more fulfilling life. The Australian composer Percy Grainger wrote some of his most deeply moving music after his mother took her life.

We so often crave happiness. However, a great deal of growth comes from the painful situations in life rather than from the happy ones. It is the discovery of our own growth emerging from these painful challenges which brings about some of the deepest happiness and which can make us truly proud of ourselves.

Viktor Frankl, the famous psychiatrist, from his own grief experiences, described these concepts of finding meaning in his book 'Man's Search for Meaning' and it's sequel 'The Will to Meaning' (see Resource list).

> *You may find fulfilment*
>
> *from accomplishing your journey*
>
> *through grief.*

The meaning in the life which your loved one lived and a new purpose for you are waiting to be discovered.

Listen to the exhortation of the dawn!

Look to this day!

For it is life, the very life of life.

In its brief course lie all the verities

and realities of your existence:

The bliss of growth,

The glory of action,

The splendour of beauty.

For yesterday is but a dream,

And tomorrow is only a vision;

But today well-lived makes every

yesterday a dream of happiness,

And every tomorrow a vision of hope.

Look well, therefore, to this day!

Such is the salutation of the dawn.

Translated from the Sanskrit.

11
What has happened to
my beliefs?

Whatever your religion, you may find bereavement alters your beliefs in some way. Everyone's experience is different. Can you identify with any of these?

*'I was furious at God that he had
allowed it to happen.'*

*'My faith supported me.
It had been tried and tested many times
before and it didn't fail me this time."*

'I totally rejected my faith to start with.'

Some have found that their religious beliefs are shattered. The foundation they thought was secure no longer exists. A major support has crumbled. This can be very scary. They wonder where they are going. What is the meaning of life; is there a God?

Many go through turmoil and searching. Some have grown up with an image of God as strongly moral and judgemental, and may find the image particularly threatening at this time. They want to reject the idea of the existence of God altogether. They may turn to other philosophies and religions.

Others see God as supportive and loving. They have found their faith is something to hang on to. It is a major support in helping them through.

> 'There was no-one I could talk to about it,
> but God was always there,'

> 'We were at our lowest point.
> If either of us had suggested we go for
> a fast drive we would have.
> Instead I picked up the book I knew best and read
> "I will lift up mine eyes unto the hills,
> from whence cometh my help.
> My help cometh from the Lord which made
> heaven and earth."
> and we are still here.'

Some people have found their personal relationship with God made the suicide of their loved one even more difficult to explain. It caused them to search for a new perspective in their faith. They needed answers to difficult questions.

> 'All my anger at God dissolved when I realised he
> was just as distressed as we were that such a terrible
> thing had happened . I realised he felt with us."

'I agonised over the thought that my son might
not go to heaven because it was he who had taken
his life. My priest told me that God would have
known how distressed my son was and would
have welcomed him, holding him in his arms
with great tenderness and love .'

'I needed the support of my counsellor desperately . It distressed me a lot that my need for help
other than God's might have been an indication
that my faith was inadequate. I felt I had failed
in my faith. Later I realised my need for help
was God's vehicle for maturing my faith.'

Through turmoil and search many people have
made discoveries in their faith, finding it grows and
develops in a way which they would never have imagined before their bereavement.

'I realised that, unfortunately, we do not grow as
people or in faith through the happy times. It is
only by plumbing the depths of despair that we
come into contact with our true selves and our
true God, and find a faith we would never have
had otherwise.'

Just as your doctor helps your physical health,
you may find it useful to see a religious counsellor about
your spiritual survival. The rituals of your religion may
also help your grief.

12

Self Care - health care

The severe stress caused by grief brings about a number of changes to the body. Glands release chemicals called hormones. These circulate in the blood stream and stimulate many parts of the body, putting them on alert. Adrenalin is one of these. In addition, the autonomic nervous system is put into overdrive. (This is a network of tiny nerve fibres which links the organs with the brain.)

These mechanisms prepare your body to cope with extreme physical and emotional effort (as in the fight or flight reaction descibed under 'Shock' in chapter 9).

Because organs such as the bowel and the heart are charged up by these mechanisms, you may experience physical symptoms: loss of appetite, nausea, abdominal pain, changed bowel habits, alteration to your normal period pattern, tremor, headaches, sleeplessness, palpitations, chest pains. These are only some of the reactions which can occur. Each person's experience is different.

If you have an on-going health condition such as diabetes or asthma, you will need to take extra care to keep it under control.

It is important that you keep your body as healthy as possible in order to avoid adding further stress. Here are a few hints.

A regular daily routine

At this time when you may feel able to live only an hour at a time, a regular routine provides structure to the day. Get up, dress, shop, walk and go to bed at regular times. Have set meal times even if you do not feel like eating.

Diet

In your state of overdrive a healthy diet is necessary to avoid running out of energy and vital nutrients, as well as keeping your stomach and bowels functioning normally.

If you lose your appetite you may find it easier to eat several small meals or snacks rather than three large meals a day. Try to include a selection from the three major food groups.

Breads and cereals (especially whole grain), fruits and vegetables all provide fibre which will help to prevent tummy pains and keep bowels regular.

If you do not feel like preparing meals, try fresh fruit, soups, yoghurt, sandwiches, cheese and biscuits. Or you can add the occasional frozen meal which only requires reheating.

Avoid fatty, salty or take-away foods. Make sure you drink at least 8 to 10 glasses of fluid a day. Milky drinks will help to keep your energy levels up, as well as being nourishing.

It is tempting to seek solace from food, too, so be equally careful not to over-indulge. This results in you becoming overweight and then unhappy about your appearance.

Exercise

Regular exercise helps you to cope better with your grief. It helps to use up some of your extra adrenalin. There is then less available to cause you troublesome symptoms such as agitation or tremor. It will also make you physically tired and help you to sleep better

69

as well as maintaining your body fitness.

Exercise also causes the release in the body of substances called endorphins. These lift the mood and make you feel better emotionally. Exercise regularly, at least three times a week. Start with a gentle walk around a park near your home. This has the additional benefit of taking you out into nature. It often calms the mind. On the other hand, you might like to take up some social sport or join a health club. If you have any doubts about your physical fitness for any of these types of exercise, consult your doctor.

Relaxation

Deep relaxation, meditation and massage may help. They relieve physical tension in the muscles and release endorphins which will lift your mood.

Various forms and methods of relaxation to choose from are; tapes for use in your home; stress management classes which may be held at your local community health centre; yoga; Tai Chi. Resources are listed in the back of this book.

Many people find nature has a tranquillising effect on the mind. Go for a walk in the bush or a park; sit and admire the sunset or an expansive view. Getting close to the forces of nature provides you with opportunity to do your grieving, to relieve your tension and to refresh your mind and spirit.

Music has a similar effect for many people.

Pets

Pets are often a great comfort in bereavement.

Animals can be very sensitive to your feelings of sadness. They will listen to everything you say and never argue! A dog always has a welcome for you when you come home. For those who live alone dogs are company and protection. Cuddling a cat or dog is very soothing. There is evidence that people with pets generally have fewer health problems.

Fun

Although it seems hard, it is important for you to spoil yourself and to make an effort to have pleasurable activities. Your mind and body are undergoing a great deal of stress. You must gain some relief at times. Do something pleasurable every day and do not allow yourself to feel guilt as your health is important.

> **SPOIL YOURSELF**
> *Walk on the beach*
> *Cuddle the cats*
> *Have a massage*
> *Visit a friend*

Sleep

Following the bereavement you will be concerned about lack of sleep. The small hours of the night are uninterrupted by the demands of daily routine and are often a valuable time for your grief work. Allowing yourself to do this will help you to progress through your grief.

Having less sleep will not do you much harm. Your body adjusts at times of grief. Sleeping tablets are unnecessary. They may even be harmful because of the risk of addiction if taken too frequently.

Try to develop a relaxing pre-sleep routine to help you get off to sleep. Listen to some relaxing music, read a light book, take a warm bath or shower, have a milk drink containing a teaspoon of sugar. A deep relaxation technique is also useful to induce sleep. Exercise during the day will make you feel physically tired at night. Good habits are the key to good sleeping patterns.

Television makes the mind alert so avoid watching it before bed. Remember, too, that tea and coffee contain caffeine which contributes to sleeplessness.

If you find you are not coping with the demands of the day because of lack of sleep, consult your doctor.

SLEEP TIPS

Daily exercise
Relaxing music
Light reading
Warm milk drink
Hot shower
No caffeine

Nightmares

These may happen at first, but usually become less frequent as time goes on. If they persist, you might find some help from a grief counsellor useful.

72

Alcohol and drugs

Alcohol and drugs blur your perception of reality and cause confusion. Although it is tempting to seek relief through drink, feelings of grief may be worsened and normal coping mechanisms lost. This will delay you on your grief journey.

Smoking

Some people try to relieve stress through smoking. This can form a bad habit which is difficult to break later, as well as being bad for your health.

Medication

It would be wonderful if the pain of grief could be solved by a tablet. Following bereavement doctors are often asked for 'something to get me through'.

Medication is not magic. It merely provides a cover-up like a bandage, rather than a cure. Some delay the grieving process. Grief experts discourage the use of many medications.

All medication has side effects. Pain-relief tablets may be harmful to your stomach. Sedatives, sleeping tablets and antidepressants may decrease your alertness and cause mental confusion.

On the other hand, medication is appropriate to alleviate certain conditions. Consult your doctor. He or she will advise you and prescribe what is most appropriate for you.

Coughs and sneezes

The immune system does not work so well in grief. You are more prone to catch infections. If you do succumb to colds, try to get more rest, drink plenty of fluids and paracetamol may help to reduce the discomfort. If you feel the symptoms are more severe, or last longer than usual, your doctor will advise the best course of action.

Concentration and forgetfulness

You may experience difficulty in concentrating on tasks. You may worry that you are becoming forgetful.

You are not losing your mind. You are preoccupied with the various emotions and tasks of grieving.

Write down things that are important to remember; lists can be very useful. Your memory will return with time.

When and why to see your doctor

• Immediately following the suicide.

This gives the opportunity to discuss any appropriate forms of help and for immediate health problems to be dealt with. It will also assist your doctor in continuing to look after you.

• Three to four months afterwards.

This is often a low point in bereavement. It is often helpful to discuss your progress at this time. Your doctor may also wish to check your blood pressure and your general health.

- To check physical symptoms.

  Should you suffer physical symptoms such as infections, for more than a few days, you should see your doctor. Chest pains and palpitations should be checked immediately.

- For practical help.

  Your GP can arrange child care, meals on wheels, a visit from a social worker, and various other forms of practical help. Your doctor can also provide certification of the cause of changes to study habits and work performance for students and workers.

- For emotional support and grief counselling.

  Your GP can help you work through some of your grief. If you wish to see the coroner's report, your doctor can request it from the coroner's office and go over it with you.

13
Some practical points

What to tell others

Many people find it extremely difficult to tell others the truth about the cause of death. They are tempted to give other reasons. This strategy may seem to ease the initial embarrassment; in the long run, though, it adds to the stress by committing them to further deception. When the truth eventually comes out there is the problem of explaining the original deception.

You may have to provide a statement about your loved one's death to the place of education or work. This may benefit you by helping you to inform a number of people at one time. It is best to give a simple statement : 'the death was caused by suicide' without going into details of how.

The information pages at the back of the book can be cut out and given to friends to help you tell them about suicide.

What to tell the children

Children may in some way feel themselves to be responsible for the suicide and need a great deal of reassurance and love. They usually know if the truth is withheld. They may learn facts from others and feel doubly rejected.

Children have the right to grieve, too. They need the opportunity to take part in all the formal ceremonies, even though they may not appear to be taking it all in.

Adults frequently worry about telling children and young people that a loved one has taken their life. They are concerned that this may appear to condone suicide as an acceptable way out of extreme difficulties. So the discussion needs to proceed further, with simple explanations that the loved one was sick and needed help but did not know how to ask.

Grasp this opportunity to discuss how and where your child or young adult could seek help if they were ever in need. Give simple straightforward information. Tell them, too, that you feel sad or angry. Make it clear that it is OK to talk about feelings. Give them lots of love and support.

Belongings

'I wish I hadn't thrown out all her things'.

In the initial turmoil people often rid themselves of all tangible reminders of the person because it hurts to see them and handle them. These belongings can be very comforting later.

Other people hold on to all their loved one's possessions for years. Giving them away at an appropriate time may help you symbolically to say goodbye to your loved one.

Making major life decisions

Many people who move house in the early part of bereavement later regret doing so. The decision frequently leads to further losses, such as friends and other supports. There is often the feeling of having left behind memories of the loved one. Some people, on the other hand, feel relieved at getting away from the place of the suicide. The decision to move should be made with consideration of possible losses. It is often not easy to anticipate these losses at the time of deep grieving. So it is usually best to delay any such major life decision until after the first anniversary.

If possible,

delay all major decisions

until after the first anniversary.

Rebuilding the family unit

You have lost one member of your family, but the family unit still remains. It is often difficult to adjust to the smaller size. But it is important to strengthen the family. Suggest dinners and outings together; give time and thought to making these special so that they may bring significant memories. Encourage your family to share in this decision-making.

Dealing with other family, friends and associates

These people may also have deep feelings of grief. Include them in your grieving and they will help you.

Dealing with Christmas and other occasions

You may fear and dread festivals which were previously times of joy; Christmas, birthdays, Mother's Day, Easter, wedding anniversaries.

These occasions remind you of happy times you enjoyed with your loved one and emphasise their absence. Usually, the worst time is the lead-up to the festival.

It is common to be concerned about how you will cope on the day itself and to dread its arrival. When the day comes it is often a relief.

It may help to spend the days before the festival planning what you will do on the day. Be positive about it. Discuss the day with your family. You may discover the strength that comes from family unity at this time.

Allow yourself time on these days to think and talk about your loved one. Light a candle, visit the grave, open a bottle of their favourite wine, play their music. They will seem closer to you, and you will treasure the depth of feeling which comes from the memories.

SURVIVING FESTIVALS

Ask yourself:

*How would my loved one wish to see me
spending the day?*

_____

_____

_____

_____

*What can I do in memory of my
loved one on this day?*

_____

_____

_____

_____

_____

Handling the anniversary

Treat it in the same way as other important days. Plan ahead. Discuss with your family how best to remember your loved one. Make sure you have someone to be with or talk to.

It is common to experience deepening grief around this time. This is followed by a feeling of release, and increasing confidence that you have managed to survive through a whole year.

It can be normal for these feelings to occur at successive anniversaries for a number of years.

The role of the coroner's office

Functions of the coronial system vary between countries and states. In Australia it is a legal requirement in all States that deaths from unnatural causes, including apparent suicide, are reported to the coroner. Police acting on behalf of the coroner investigate and document each death that is reported. The purpose is to determine the manner, cause and circumstances surrounding the death.

There is an educational and preventive function inherent in the coronial system. The coroner is permitted to make recommendations which may lessen the likelihood of a similar event happening again.

Medical reports

A post-mortem examination is performed by a pathologist to establish the medical cause of death.

The report may be made available to the next of

kin once the investigations have been completed. This may take several months.

States vary in providing access to information. In many States the coroner's report or a summary is sent to the family or their nominated medical practitioner (usually the family doctor) on request.

The doctor may help the family deal with the issues and explain and discuss any complex medical information. Any request for a report should be made in writing and forwarded to the coroner's office, giving name and address of the doctor or person requesting it, and the details of the deceased, including the date of death.

Counselling and support services at the coroner's office

States vary in provision of counselling by the coroner's office and may include; support if needed, especially during the time immediately following the death; information about the coronial system; information relating to any notes that may have been written prior to the death. More information can be obtained by contacting your State office (see Resource list).

14
Some business and financial points

*'I managed OK for the first few days and then
everything seemed to get on top of me. I forgot the
mortgage payment and the electricity bill. Then I
didn't do anything about the parking fine and
the car registration was forgotten . . .'*

The trouble is you may be in no fit state to organise anything. Your financial contacts do not know of your tragedy. Your bank manager, for instance, needs to be told what has happened and how it affects you. Unless arrangements are made to handle your financial matters until you are able to resume some semblance of a normal life, you may end up in very hot water with the power or telephone cut off, threatened repossession of your car, mortgage foreclosure . . .

If you cannot inform creditors and suppliers yourself, ask a friend, accountant or minister of religion to do it. Give them details of all the commitments and payments you can think of. Ask them to write to the companies explaining why payments may be irregular for a while. This gives you a breathing space while you sort out more permanent arrangements.

FINANCIAL CHECKLIST
Electricity
Gas
Mortgage
Loans
Insurance
Telephone
Car Registration
Rates
Credit Card Facilities
Regular Payments

_____

_____

_____

If you need time to organise your affairs, use holiday leave. Also, find out how much sick leave you have owing and arrange to use some of that as well. (Keep some up your sleeve in case of more unforeseen problems).

Discuss sick leave with your GP who should be able to provide you with a certificate.

Spend a short time each week going through your mail to ensure that any financial letters are dealt with. This helps the healing process, too, and is an important step in keeping you in contact with reality.

Income protection policies

If you are unable to perform your normal standard of work, so reducing your income, the policy may be called on to provide cover. You will need a medical certificate stating the cause; eg 'intense grief causing . . .'. Insurance companies may need some persuasion to accept your case as genuine, but most policies cover this type of claim.

Loss of main income

If you have lost your main income earner, contact a financial adviser. Ask your friends for a recommendation. An accountant with expertise in this area can be found through telephoning one of the professional bodies listed in the yellow pages or the resource list of this book.

Alternatively your bank manager may be able to help. General financial counsellors or share brokers are listed in the yellow pages. Money spent on financial advice may save you a great deal in the long run.

Insurance policies

These need to be checked and called in. Be prepared for some refusals because of the manner of death.

Some policies may exclude suicide as a claimable event. Feeling angry at the companies is normal. It might help you, but the person at the other end of the phone is not experiencing your grief and is only doing their job!

Finally

Don't make any life-changing financial decisions at this time without consulting a financial adviser.

If you have any doubts about anything financial during this traumatic and lonely period be prepared to pass the burden on to a trusted friend or adviser. Do not ignore anything financial.

15
You are not alone -
some facts about suicide

Suicide has always been one of the greatest tragedies of society. Every year nearly one million people world wide take their lives. There are estimated to be at least six close family members and friends associated with each person who takes their life who are left with intense grief. This means that each year six million people are bereaved through suicide.

There are around 4500 suicides a year in England and Wales, over 30 000 a year in the United States, and 2000 in Australia.

The suicide rate in the USA, Canada, Australia and New Zealand is the same at about 13 per 100 000 of population. The rate is a little lower in the United Kingdom. Some countries, however, have a far greater suicide rate. For example, Hungary's rate is four times that of any of these countries.

The rate of youth suicide is high in Australia and New Zealand, and is rising in the United Kingdom. In most English speaking countries there is a peak in middle age and, except for the United Kingdom, an even higher peak in the elderly.

The statistics, though, are an underestimate. Unless suicide can be proven, the death is recorded as 'misadventure' or 'accidental'. Some single car accidents and drug overdoses may be suicides but never proven.

In most countries, suicide is among the ten leading causes of death and in the young, suicide and road fatalities are the two major causes.

Although women more frequently make attempts on their lives, completed suicide is three times more common in males.

FACTS ABOUT SUICIDE
1 million suicides worldwide each year
6 million bereaved world wide each year
Commonest in males
Occurs in all social classes

Certain risk factors for suicide have been identified but they are too many and too non-specific to accurately identify those who will take their lives. One specialist tried to predict those who would take their lives from 4800 people whom he identified as being at risk.

He incorrectly identified 1200 whom he thought would kill themselves but did not. He also missed thirty two who later killed themselves, and correctly identified only thirty five who eventually did take their lives.

Unfortunately, despite thousands of dollars spent on suicide research, progress in prediction is painfully slow.

16
Finally . . .

You may find it hard to believe now but your grief will not stay the same. It will change as you work through it and you will come to feel more comfortable about your loss. If you so choose, you may grow as a person from the experience and integrate that experience into your existence and create a more meaningful life for yourself and others. In effect, the influence of your loved one will still live on.

Suicide bereavement
support groups

Australia

South Australia

Bereaved Through Suicide
Support Group
PO Box 151
Kent Town
South Australia 5071
Contact: Service Information
Line (08) 8332 8240

Victoria

'Spring'
Our Lady of Assumption
Church
9 Centre Dandenong Road
Cheltenham
Victoria 3192
Contact: Kathleen Crawford
(03) 9521 6567 or
(03) 9585 0272

Tasmania

Dorset Support Group
C/o 73 Ringarooma Road
Legerwood
Tasmania 7261
Contact: Dot Ranson
(03) 6353 2255

New South Wales

Bereaved by Suicide Support
Group
Salvation Army
Cnr Johnson & Archer Streets,
Chatswood
PO Box 687
Chatswood
New South Wales 2057
Contact: David Collison:
(02) 9419 8695

Bereaved by Suicide Support
Group
PO Box 1661
Ashfield
New South Wales 1800
Contact: Elsa or Erik:
(02) 9419 4135

Central Coast Area Mental
Health Services
C/o Gosford Hospital
PO Box 361
Gosford
New South Wales 2250
Contact: Mark Joyce/Susan
Syddall: (02) 4320 3170

Queensland

Survivors of Suicide Group
9 Harvey Street
Gladstone
Queensland 4680
Contact: Lynda Stephens:
(079) 781 843 or
Shirley Deno: (079) 781 583

Suicide Survivors Support
Group
19 Mount Peter Road
Edmonton
Queensland 4869
Contact: Fran: (07) 4045 2955

Western Australia

Survivors of Suicide Support
Group
Samaritan House
60 Bagot Street
Subiaco
Western Australia 6008
Contact: Samaritans:
(08) 9381 5555

Further information may be
obtained from your state
branch of the National
Association for Loss and Grief
(see Resource List).

New Zealand

Listings of support groups may
be obtained from:

NALAG New Zealand
PO Box 166
Waiuku
South Aukland

United Kingdom

Belfast: 01232 232 695
Cambridge: 01223 302 662
Scotland: 0131 551 1511
Glasgow: 0141 248 2199
Ivel Beds: 01767 312 997
London: 0345 585 565
Winchester: 01962 885 562
Epsom: 01372 745 077

Survivors of Bereavement by
Suicide (SOBS)
Beverley: 01964 537 191
Cheshire: 01925 752 932
Chislehurst: 0181 467 7081
Chesterfield: 01246 866 175
Cornwall: 01566 782 200
Oxford: 01235 863 060
Hull: 01482 565 387
Leicestershire: 01530 415 307
Norfolk: 01953 887 494
Solihull: 0121 704 4298
Jersey: 01534 37513

Further listings may be
obtained from:

Compassionate Friends
Shadow of Suicide Support
Groups
53 North Street
Briston BS3 1EN
Tel 0117 953 9639

Cruse Bereavement Care
126 Sheen Road
Richmond
Surrey TW9 1UR
Tel 0181 940 4818

National Association of
Bereavement Services
Helpline 0171 247 1080

Samaritans:
Tel 0345 909 090 (national no)
Ipswich: 01473 211 133
Croydon: 0181 681 6666
Norwich: 01603 611 311

United States of America

Listings of support groups may
be obtained from:

American Association of
Suicidology
4201 Connecticut Avenue, NW
Suite 310
Washington DC 20008
USA
Tel (202) 237 2280
Fax (202) 237 2282
Website:
www.cyberpsych.org/aas

Suicide Prevention Centre, Inc.
PO Box 1393
Dayton OH 45401-1393
USA
Contact: Crisis Line: 297 4777
Business Office: 297 9096

Canada

Listings of support groups may
be obtained from:

Suicide Information and
Education Centre
201, 1615 10th Avenue SW
Calgary
Alberta T3C 0J7
e-mail: seic@seic.ca
website: http://www.siec.ca
phone: (403) 245 3900
fax: (403) 245 0299

Resource list

Books

Clarke, Jack, Life after Grief: a soul journey after suicide. Personal Pathways Press, Georgia, USA. *A man's struggle following his wife's suicide.*

Colgrove, Bloomfield and McWilliams, How to Survive the Loss of a Love. Bantam Books, Sydney. *Fifty-eight practical points to survival.*

Fabian, Suzane, The Last Taboo: suicide among children and adolescents. Penguin Books Australia Ltd, Ringwood, Victoria. *A comprehensive book about suicide in the young.*

Frankl, Viktor, Man's Search for Meaning. Hodder and Stoughton, Rydalmere, NSW. *Frankl's own experience of his time in Auschwitz and his personal philosophy of surviving loss.*

Frankl, Viktor, The Will to Meaning. New American Library, New York. *A continuation of Frankl's philosophy.*

Lord, Janice Harris, No Time for Goodbyes. Millennium Press, Sydney. *Looks at reactions of different family members following death from various tragic circumstances.*

Hayward, Susan, A Guide for the Advanced Soul: bag of jewels. In-Tune Books, Avalon NSW. *An anthology of thoughts to ponder.*

Jampolsky, Gerald, Goodbye to Guilt. Bantam Books, Sydney. *A gentle book to finding peace.*

Keating, Kathleen, The First Book of Hugs. Angus & Robertson Publishers, North Ryde, NSW. *A humorous and illustrated guide to one method of promoting feelings of well-being.*

Kushner, Harold, When Bad Things Happen to Good People. Pan Books, London. *Rabbi Kuschner deals with tragedy.*

Lukas, Christopher and Seiden, Henry, Silent Grief: living in the wake of suicide. Papermac, London. *A guide to survival written by a man who experienced multiple suicides in his family, together with the psychologist who helped him through.*

McKissock, Mal, Coping with Grief. Australian Broadcasting Corporation Enterprises, Sydney. *A concise handbook on grief.*

Meares, Ainslie, Relief without Drugs. Fontana-Collins, Glasgow, UK. *A self-help book of relaxation for conquering tension, pain and anxiety.*

Seamands, David A, Healing for Damaged Emotions. Victor Books, Wheaton, Illinios, USA.
A Christian approach to healing.

Scott Peck M, The Road Less Travelled. Simon and Schuster, New York.
A book on personal development.

Wertheimer, Alison, A Special Scar: the experiences of people bereaved by suicide. Tavistock/Routledge, London.
An excellent further text about the experiences of suicide bereavement from one who has been there.

Creative Thoughts: peace and quiet. Creative Publishing; Bath, UK.
Another anthology of thoughts to ponder.

Tapes

Foundation Studios, 'Suicide: The Ultimate Rejection.' Women's and Children's Hospital, North Adelaide, South Australia 5006.
A videotape in which some bereaved people and helping professionals of a support group talk about their experiences.

Foundation Studios, 'Suicide: Some Years down the Track.' Women and Children's Hospital, North Adelaide, South Australia 5006.
A videotape of interviews with bereaved people several years after the suicide of a loved one.

Ritchie, Jan, 'Relaxation and Stress Management.' New South Wales Dept of Health, (available from major chemists).
An audiotape giving practical exercises in relaxation.

McKissock, Mal, 'Coping with Grief.' Australian Broadcasting Corporation Enterprises, Sydney.
An audiotape of the book.

Other resources

Crisis counselling services

Lifeline and other telephone counselling services can be located in the front of your local telephone directory under 'Community Help Reference'.
Other services include:
Your doctor;
Hospital accident & emergency departments;
Your local community health centre.

Grief counsellors

Your funeral director, local community health centre, GP or state branch of the National Association of Loss and Grief will be able to make suitable recommendations.

Bereavement Education

Classes about loss and grief are held by some funeral directors. The funeral director with whom you had contact will direct you to the nearest bereavement education centre.

National Association of Loss and Grief

For further information about support groups, bereavement education classes, grief counselling, and literature.

South Australia	(08) 8411 3124
New South Wales	(02) 9988 3376
Victoria & Tasmania	(03) 9331 3555
Western Australia	(09) 9497 7251
ACT	(02) 6291 4994

Accounting organisations

Australia

See your local telephone directory for listings of:

Australian Society of Certified Practising Accountants;
The Institute of Chartered Accountants in Australia;
National Institute of Accountants.

United Kingdom

The Institute of Chartered Accountants in England and Wales
The Chartered Association of Certified Accountants

United States of America

American Institute of Certified Public Accountants
National Association of State Boards of Accountants

Coroner's offices in Australia:

South Australia	(08) 8204 0600
Northern Territory	(08) 8999 7597
Western Australia	(08) 9321 2491
New South Wales	(02) 9552 4066
Tasmania	(03) 6233 2020
Queensland	(07) 3247 4606
Victoria	(03) 9684 4444
ACT	(02) 6217 4400

ABOUT SUICIDE

Suicide is a great tragedy. Nearly one million people world wide take their lives each year.

We do not know exactly what causes suicide. Social pressures and personality have been implicated. Suicide has caused the death of many morally aware, sensitive, caring and artistic individuals. Gifted artists, writers and poets have taken their lives; Vincent van Gogh, Virginia Woolf, Tony Hancock and Adam Lindsay Gordon. Was the stress of life too much for these sensitive souls?

Doctors have recognised for a long time that nearly all who take their lives have suffered a mental illness. Evidence is emerging for physical causes for such illness, and also for suicide. Just as in diabetes insulin in the body is low so that it cannot regulate sugar, before suicide, serotonin, a chemical in the brain, reaches a critical level. So the mind cannot properly control thoughts. These changes may be related to severe stress.

It can be very difficult to recognise at the time anything wrong with the person, as changes in behaviour develop gradually.

Therefore suicide may be regarded as the consequence of a physical illness affecting the brain, although social and personal factors may also play a part. Much more research is needed to accurately diagnose and prevent suicide.

Helping friends and relatives
who have been bereaved through suicide.

People who have lost a loved one through suicide are left feeling very hurt, confused and alone. They have feelings of shock, guilt and rejection. These feelings will continue for them long after your own grief has healed. You may wish to know how you can help them. This information may give you a guide.

The news of suicide may shock you greatly and you and your own circle of family and friends may have difficulty dealing with it. You may find it helpful to talk about it among yourselves. This will benefit you in helping the grieving friend or family. Helping them will not put your family at risk of suicide. More information is available in the book this leaflet came from. Ask your friend or relative to lend it to you.

Permission to photocopy.

Helping the bereaved

What will help	What won't help
Spend time and really listen.	Avoiding talking about the loss.
Let them know that what they are experiencing is normal.	Inhibiting them by offering advice.
Encourage expressions of feelings in their own way.	Lectures or reason.
Accept their behaviour - crying, screaming, being quiet, laughing.	Expecting or judging how it should be.
Empathise - empathy is the basis of a helping relationship.	Using clichés.
Try to understand and accept this person. Everyone is different.	False reassurance.
Allow expressions of anger, guilt and blame. Reflect on the meaning of their words. Let them know you understand what they are saying.	Saying, 'I know how you feel'.
	Trying to do everything for them.
Indicate that grief takes time.	Trivialising their loss.
Maintain contact personally or by telephone. Visits need not be long.	Comparing other losses.
	Describing the theory of grief.
Give hugs where appropriate.	Taking the focus away from what they are saying.
Talk about the lost person.	Interpreting.
Include children in family grieving.	Putting your feelings on to their situation.
	Dropping the person if the going gets heavy.
	Giving details of your grief.

National Association for Loss and Grief (NSW). Adapted with permission

> *Give:*
> *a good ear;*
> *time to listen;*
> *a hug (where appropriate).*
>
> *Maintain contact.*

from: Clark, Sheila: 'After Suicide: help for the bereaved'.
Hill of Content Publishing Co. Pty Ltd, Melbourne, Australia.